50 Things to Know

50 THINGS TO KNOW ABOUT COPING WITH STRESS

By A Mental Health Specialist

Kimberly L. Brownridge
LMHC, LPC, NCC, CTMH

50 Things to Know About Coping with Stress Copyright © 2020 by CZYK Publishing LLC.
All Rights Reserved.

All rights reserved. No part of this book may be reproduced in any form or by any electronic or mechanical means including information storage and retrieval systems, without permission in writing from the author. The only exception is by a reviewer, who may quote short excerpts in a review.

The statements in this book are of the authors and may not be the views of CZYK Publishing or 50 Things to Know.
Cover designed by: Ivana Stamenkovic
Cover Image: https://pixabay.com/photos/alone-sad-depression-lonely-4672965/
Editor: Ambre Lane

CZYK Publishing Since 2011.

50 Things to Know

Lock Haven, PA
All rights reserved.
ISBN: 9798557712903

50 THINGS TO KNOW BOOK SERIES REVIEWS FROM READERS

I recently downloaded a couple of books from this series to read over the weekend thinking I would read just one or two. However, I so loved the books that I read all the six books I had downloaded in one go and ended up downloading a few more today. Written by different authors, the books offer practical advice on how you can perform or achieve certain goals in life, which in this case is how to have a better life.

The information is simple to digest and learn from, and is incredibly useful. There are also resources listed at the end of the book that you can use to get more information.

50 Things To Know To Have A Better Life: Self-Improvement Made Easy!

Author Dannii Cohen

This book is very helpful and provides simple tips on how to improve your everyday life. I found it to be useful in improving my overall attitude.

50 Things to Know For Your Mindfulness & Meditation Journey
Author Nina Edmondso

Quick read with 50 short and easy tips for what to think about before starting to homeschool.

50 Things to Know About Getting Started with Homeschool by Author Amanda Walton

I really enjoyed the voice of the narrator, she speaks in a soothing tone. The book is a really great reminder of things we might have known we could do during stressful times, but forgot over the years.

Author Harmony Hawaii

There is so much waste in our society today. Everyone should be forced to read this book. I know I am passing it on to my family.

50 Things to Know to Downsize Your Life: How To Downsize, Organize, And Get Back to Basics

Author Lisa Rusczyk Ed. D.

Great book to get you motivated and understand why you may be losing motivation. Great for that person who wants to start getting healthy, or just for you when you need motivation while having an established workout routine.

50 Things To Know To Stick With A Workout: Motivational Tips To Start The New You Today

Author Sarah Hughes

50 Things to Know About Coping with Stress

BOOK DESCRIPTION

Has stress taken over your life, and you don't know what to do? Do you ever wonder why we have to feel stressed? Are you ready to find the best coping skills for handling stress? If you answered yes to any of these questions, then this book is for you.

50 Things to Know About Coping with Stress by Kimberly L. Brownridge offers an approach to coping with stress that other books don't. Most books on stress provide a list of coping skills to try. Although there's nothing wrong with that, they never explain how to implement these coping skills into our lives. Based on experience and strong clinical background, Kimberly takes the time to explain the steps to try new coping skills and provide some examples.

In these pages, you'll discover what stress is and which coping skills are most beneficial. This book will help you eliminate destructive coping skills and implement constructive coping skills.

By the time you finish this book, you will have a new inventory of coping skills to choose from when struggling with a stressful event. So grab YOUR copy today. You'll be glad you did.

TABLE OF CONTENTS

50 Things to Know
Book Series
Reviews from Readers
BOOK DESCRIPTION
TABLE OF CONTENTS
ABOUT THE AUTHOR
INTRODUCTION
1. What Is Stress
2. Causes of Stress
3. Stress Is Normal
4. Signs of Stress
5. Stress and Health
6. Stress and Mental Health
7. Coping Skills
8. Purpose of Coping Skills
9. Coping Skills Are Learned
10. Types of Coping Skills

Destructive Coping Skills
11. Stress Eating
12. Stress Starving
13. Risky Sexual Behaviors
14. Drugs and Alcohol
15. Violent Behaviors

16. Criminal Behavior
17. Giving Up
18. Virtual Escape
19. Self-Harm/Self-Injury
20. Suicide

Constructive Coping Skills
21. Positive Attitude
22. Relaxation
23. Exercise
24. Eat Healthy
25. Time Management
26. Hobbies
27. Rest
28. Social Support
29. Journaling/Vlogging
30. Art Creativity
31. Music & Dance
32. Gardening
33. Nature
34. Emotional Support Animal
35. Aromatherapy/Essential Oils
36. Books/Movies
37. Bath/Shower
38. Stress Toys
39. Laugh

40. Smile & Breathe
41. Reframed Thinking
42. Initial Perspective
43. Alternate Perspective
44. Find Resolution
45. Be Grateful
46. Prayer/Meditation
47. Seek Professional Help
48. Kids & Stress
49. Family Time
50. Family Photos
51. Pep Talks
52. Extended Family & Friends
Other Helpful Resources
50 Things to Know

ABOUT THE AUTHOR

Kimberly L. Brownridge is an African-American, Licensed Professional Counselor (LPC), Licensed Mental Health Counselor (LMHC), National Certified Counselor (NCC), and Certified Clinical Telemental Health Provider (CTMH). She has a MA in Professional Counseling and MS in General Psychology. Kimberly maintains a small private practice, Counsel The Mind, LLC, providing traditional therapy and online therapy. Her areas of specialty are stress management, couple relationship/marriage, teen issues, LGBTQ, and depression & anxiety.

She has been an educator in the field of psychology for over ten years and currently teaches at Marian University, University of the People, and Myrtle Beach Wesleyan College/Pilgrim Seminary. Her goal is to continue her career writing books. The next books she is working on is about teaching young woman life lessons she has learned over the years.

She currently resides in Indiana where she actively volunteers at her children's school, School Commission and Class Parent Rep. The most important people in her life are her children, and her dog, Guinness, is very special too.

You can find her at
https://www.betterhelp.com/kimberly-brownridge/
Linked-In: kimberlydaviebrownridge

ABOUT THE EDITOR

Ambre Lane, proprietor of FastLane Editing, was born to help writers. She currently lives in Avon, Indiana with her three children and 3 pets. She buys a ridiculous amount of food. When she was a mere 13 years old, she got her first job as an editor for her school newspaper. She has not stopped editing since. She devours books at an unbelievable rate just for fun, even winning a bet in 2020 that she could read 100 novels in less than 100 days (she did it in 33). Since then she has been the go-to person at every school and job to perfect everything from emails to doctoral dissertations. In 2019, she formally established FastLane Editing. Relying on her degrees in business management and communication and as a Certified Associate in Project Management (CAPM), she is continuing to help others make their writing the best it could be. If you need an editor for your writing, find her at FastLaneA@protonmail.com.

INTRODUCTION

Stress is one thing that universally affects everyone. The main problem with stress is that most people do not know how to handle it. The ability to cope with stress is an essential life skill that should be taught. However, to teach good coping skills, one must possess good coping skills. Parents often have poor coping skills, so they teach their children poor coping skills, and the cycle continues.

Learning and understanding as much as we can about stress and coping skills makes it easier to navigate life. There are hundreds of unique coping skills that assist with daily life stressors. Some can become unique to the person, and some are universal. Taking the time to determine what works for us is the step most people skip.

This book will give the opportunity to explore different coping skills and learn how to implement them. Every coping skill listed will not work for everyone. A significant start to this journey will be to find 3 to 5 coping skills that offer us relief from the stressful events in our life.

1. WHAT IS STRESS

Stress is our body's emotional, mental, and physical reaction to a challenging event. An event could be a situation, environment, thought, person, anything. This emotional, mental, and physical reaction brings tension or strain on our bodies. We dislike a sense, so we will do whatever we can to make this feeling go away.

A prominent example of an event is the global COVID-19 pandemic. The pandemic caused many people a sizeable amount of stress worldwide. Isolation from loved ones and having to quarantine themselves has mentally affected countless people. Others have been affected physically by the actual COVID-19 virus. Last, many have been shaken emotionally with the constant worry and fear of contracting the COVID-19 virus or the difficulties of loved ones who have.

Again, our natural reaction is to fight against and resist the feelings of stress. Stress is a routine part of life. Our body reacts to all stimulation that crosses our path. A hard life lesson is to recognize that we cannot control everything and that some things are completely out of our command. We cannot control whether stress comes into our lives, but we can control how we handle it.

2. CAUSES OF STRESS

Since stress is an unavoidable aspect of life, there are limitless causes. Stress usually has a trigger, called a stimulus, that causes a specific feeling or emotion, that causes the mind and/or body to react. We are all different, so we all have different triggers. What triggers you may not trigger someone else. One big event or several minor events that gradually build pressure over time can triggered Stress.

There are many reasons behind why specific triggers cause stress while others do not. One factor is the personal perception of a specific situation. If you are the person who sees situations as the glass is half empty, then any situation that is not going your way could become a trigger of stress. Another factor that will determine if an event will cause you stress is the amount of pressure on you at that moment. If you already have five balls in the air, then a new ball is added or a new event, you will be more likely to be triggered for stress. Resilience is another factor, how easily you bounce back from difficulties and disappointments in your life. If moving forward after a disappointment is challenging for you, stress responses could be easily triggered. Lastly, your support system is a significant factor in determining your triggers for stress. If you do not have friends and family that support you and help you during times of stress, you will be more susceptible to many triggers.

Events in life triggering stress:
- extreme pressure
- life changes
- constant worrying
- lack of control
- feelings of uncertainty

3. STRESS IS NORMAL

Stress is a natural part of life, and it serves a purpose. No one is promised a problem-free existence, but that is our expectation. So, problems, changes and disruption to our daily routine bring about stress. Stress is not always bad. Even though stress is unpleasant, it can keep us safe. Stress motivates us to leave an unpleasant situation. Stress activates our fight-or-flight response.

Scientifically, when stressed, our body's sympathetic nervous system is activated because of a sudden release of hormones. Hormones such as cortisol and adrenaline which force us into action to do something about the stressful event.

We are designed to handle stressful events. Stress dates back to biblical times, such as Adam's reactions about eating from the forbidden tree with Eve. Stress is here to stay, which makes it imperative that we know how to handle it.

4. SIGNS OF STRESS

We all exhibit stress differently. However, there are some universal signs of stress. Sometimes the signs are apparent from the beginning, but other times it may take a while. Stress affects our behavior, emotions, and physical health.

Behavior Signs:
- Appetite changes - eating more or less than usual
- Nervousness - fidgeting, hair pulling, nail-biting, pacing
- Drug or alcohol use or abuse
- Socialization changes - withdrawal from others or over partying Sleep changes - too much or too little

Emotional Signs:
- Sadness or depression
- Anger or irritability
- Loneliness or hopelessness
- Anxiety or agitation
- Worsened symptoms of mental illness

Physical Health Signs:
- Headaches
- Changes in breathing - shallow or hyperventilating
- Chest pain or indigestion
- Sickness - vomiting, bowel issues, inability to fight off a virus
- High Blood Pressure

AND MUCH MORE...

5. STRESS AND HEALTH

The human body is designed to handle stress. However, everything has a threshold, and once the stress threshold is exceeded, there is an adverse reaction. Acute physical or mental suffering for a prolonged period without relief can lead to chronic stress disorder. Distress can contribute to several health issues such as diabetes, heart disease, ulcers, high blood pressure, sexual dysfunction, and more.

Stress is one of the leading causes of untimely death. Stress is normal, but chronic stress can be deadly. A person dealing with chronic stress is three times more likely to die prematurely. While unlikely to just drop dead in the middle of stressful situations because the stress was too much, a stressful situation could be too much for our heart, causing a heart attack. It could exhaust or overwork our adrenal glands so that the cortisol hormone causes our body the inability to self-regulate or could cause blood clots that travel to the brain, causing a stroke.

Stress can be a motivator or a murderer. We decide the role stress plays in our life.

6. STRESS AND MENTAL HEALTH

Stress can be as hazardous to our mental health as it to our medical health. Stress is a gateway to several mental disorders such as depression, anxiety, substance abuse, psychosis, sleep disorders, and more. It also causes memory problems, attention deficits, emotional outbursts and difficulties relating to others. Logical thought is also at risk with stress.

The ability to think clearly and logically is crucial. The average person makes approximately 35,000 decisions in a day. If we are not thinking clearly, how can we make the right choice from minute-to-minute or hour-to-hour?

So many of us worry that when we have these struggles, we are losing our mind or have a mental disorder. Majority of the time stress is the culprit. We must learn how to handle stress in a positive way in order to maintain our sanity and peace of mind.

7. COPING SKILLS

The essential life skill that so many of us never learned is how to COPE. To cope is the ability to solve, minimize, or tolerate the problems of stress in one's life with coping skills. We learn how to cope in childhood by absorbing the actions of adults present in our life. Unfortunately, many of the adults in our life never learned to use constructive cope skills either, which leaves us with a vicious cycle of people growing up unable to cope with all the trials and tribulations in their lives.

We were never promised that life would be easy or without obstacles. To survive this roller coaster we call life, we need to have coping skills. Coping skills are the actions or methods one takes to deal with stress. We are different in what causes us stress; we are also different in the coping skills that relieve our stress. Also, copings skills work differently depending on the situation. Deep breathing exercises may help with stress at home, but not necessarily with work stress. We should have five to ten coping skills in our repertoire.

> *"The greatest weapon against stress is our ability to choose one thought over another."*
>
> ~William James

8. PURPOSE OF COPING SKILLS

Resiliency is the goal. When we experience a traumatic event, we want to have the skills to bounce back. Coping skills are the key to becoming resilient. Coping skills are the techniques and devices we need to adapt to the tragedies and traumas we experience. Our coping skills get us from moment to moment during the most challenging times.

The hardest part about tragedy and trauma is trying to function amid the pain (physical and/or emotional), confusion, fear and demands surrounding us. Coping skills can be the anchor we hold on to during the chaos. They keep us functioning from minute-to-minute, hour-to-hour, day to day, and so on. The more we practice navigating the chaos, the better we become at coping, then we become resilient.

> *"Our greatest glory is not in never failing, but in rising up every time we fail."*
>
> ~ Ralph Waldo Emerson

9. COPING SKILLS ARE LEARNED

So many people say, "I don't have any coping skills," "My family says my coping skills are bad," or "My coping skills do not work." Most of us do not realize that we learn our coping skills from watching others, specifically our parents. As we grow up, we see our parents struggle with daily stressors. Then we watch how they handle it, and we try to do the same when we are stressed. Sometimes what we learn is helpful to us, and sometimes it is not.

If we see our mother grab a bottle of alcohol whenever something stressed her, we are more prone to reach for alcohol when stressed; even if we notice it does not help mom. Similarly, if we see our father grab the bible whenever he was stressed, we will most likely reach for the bible when stressed. We will often stick to specific coping skills just because our parents did it, whether or not it is beneficial to us.

As we mature, we should take the best coping skills learned from our parents and incorporate them with other coping skills we learn over time from others or just life experiences. The stronger our coping skills are, the stronger generations to come will be.

> *"A setback is a setup for a comeback."*
>
> ~Willie Jolley

10. TYPES OF COPING SKILLS

Coping skills are the approaches and tools we need to adapt to tragedies and traumas we experience. These techniques can be positive or negative.

Destructive coping skills may seem like they help us in the short-term, but they are barriers to positive outcomes we are striving for in the long-term. Destructive coping skills, like substance abuse, usually only provide us with temporary relief. Once the temporary relief subsides, the problem remains.

Destructive coping skills do not offer what we require to resolve the issue at hand. These coping skills lead to more tragedy, trauma, and stress.

Constructive coping skills do all the things that destructive coping skills do not. They provide what we need to fix the issue at hand. They give us tools that work in the short-term and the long-term, like journaling. Sometimes it is harder to choose constructive coping skills because it takes more effort. To survive in today's world, we cannot rely on instant gratification and temporary fixes. To be resilient, we must exercise winning techniques.

> *"It's not stress that kills us, it's our reaction to it."*
>
> ~Hans Selye

DESTRUCTIVE COPING SKILLS

11. STRESS EATING

Many of us use food as a crutch when stressed, whether it is an excess of food or lack. We use food to fill an emotional void instead of filling our belly when stressed. When we eat foods we crave, our brain releases the chemical dopamine. Dopamine is a drug our body naturally produces. Dopamine helps us to feel pleasure and satisfaction in our life. Food can provide temporary joy and relief from stress while eating, so it seems like a constructive coping skill. However, stress eating causes a host of other problems. Stress eating can start a vicious cycle:

feeling stressed --> having cravings or food urges --> eating to fill emotional void --> feeling guilty about overeating --> feeling stress all over again

It can also lead to obesity, health problems, and an inappropriate relationship with food and eating. Eating when we are not hungry increases our calorie intake, which leads to gaining weight and obesity. Overeating can cause high blood pressure which can lead to heart problems, diabetes, high cholesterol and so many other illnesses. Some of these illnesses can lead to premature death. We want a good relationship with food since we need food to live. No one wants to feel guilt or shame whenever it is time to eat. Like most things, eating, even our cravings, are good in moderation.

> *"The pause, even simply a breath, taken between hunger and eating, is the first step toward taking control."*
>
> ~Melissa McCreery

12. STRESS STARVING

Overeating to cope with stress is not healthy, and neither is starving to cope with stress. When we starve ourselves, it is more about control versus weight concerns. We are looking for peace amid chaos. If we feel we cannot control the chaos, we find something we can control, such as eating habits. Again, finding some control gives us temporary relief, but it does not solve the real problem.

Like overeating, starving can lead to a host of other problems. Our lean muscle mass and the size of our organs decrease. Starvation affects the brain functioning, blood pressure and the heart, causes chronic fatigue, adversely affects sexual function, and so much more. We all want control over what happens to us, but the reality is there are things out of our command. We cannot always control the stressful chaos so, let us control the coping skills we use to survive.

> *"Let go of toxic control, in order to regain healthy control."*
>
> ~ Kayla Rose Kotecki

13. RISKY SEXUAL BEHAVIORS

We all know that sex can be a great stress reliever. However, it is imperative to practice safe sex. Similar to when we eat foods we crave, when having sex, we release endorphins and other hormones that elevate our pleasure. Now, when feeling stressed, having sex with the next attractive person we pass is not the best way to relieve the pressure.

Risky sexual behaviors can include:

- Multiple sexual partners simultaneously
- Unprotected sex (including oral and anal) without a condom
- High-risk partners (drug users, partners with many partners)
- Sex at a young age
- Sex trade work

Unsafe sex may relieve the stress, but it can also bring new stressors, such as sexually transmitted diseases, HIV, and pregnancy. Sex is not about just preventing births anymore; it is about preventing deaths. Stress can be challenging and painful, but we do not want to be on our death bed wishing we had chosen a better way to handle that specific stressful situation. If we are going to use sex as a coping skill, let us make sure we are having sex with our one committed partner.

"Safe sex is an act of self-love."

~Miya Yamanouchi

14. DRUGS AND ALCOHOL

Drugs and alcohol allow us to escape mentally from our life temporarily. We also call this form of coping self-medicating. The pain and the struggle disappear, so it seems. Drugs and alcohol alter how we think and feel, so the stressful event does not seem so bad, or we do not acknowledge it at all. This is precisely what we need at that moment, but again, this relief is only temporary. Once we are sober, the stressful event is still sitting there waiting.

Like most destructive coping skills, drugs and alcohol are bad for our health. Using drugs and alcohol to cope with stress can lead to addiction. Addiction is a disease that affects the brain. Addiction can cause the body to crave drugs and alcohol, even when we are not stressed. This causes a whole new stressful event.

"GOD grant me the serenity to accept the things I cannot change, courage to change the things I can, and wisdom to know the difference."

~Serenity Prayer

15. VIOLENT BEHAVIORS

The metaphor "Kick the Dog" has been used loosely and comically in our society for decades. This means that when we are stressed, we take our frustrations out on others that are weaker than us or that are not the source of our frustrations. Violent behavior can seem like a great way to release tension and to let it be known it upsets us. However, our temporary relief causes stress to others, specifically those we care for the most. There is a constructive way to use violent behaviors to relieve stress. To cope, we can express these behaviors in a controlled environment, such as a boxing class, becoming a mixed martial arts fighter, beating up the pillow alone in the room, going to a rage room (a place designed for destruction), and including fighting equipment in the home gym. These options prevent the physical and emotional abuse of loved ones (including pets).

Domestic violence, abuse, assault, and bullying all stem from violent behaviors used as coping mechanisms to stress. When we are stressed, we sometimes behave differently than usual. However, this does not give us the right to hurt others because we are hurting. The temporary relief that violent behaviors provide is so brief we do not feel it most times. As a coping skill, violent behaviors usually end up with hospitalizations, jail/prison time, and ultimately being alone.

> *"If you want to change attitudes, start with a change in behavior."*
>
> ~Katharine Hepburn

16. CRIMINAL BEHAVIOR

We have all made many mistakes in our lives, especially when we were young. There is a reason the phrase "Young & Dumb" is so popular. Choosing criminal behaviors to get by with stress is not defined by age, but many of us considered or chose this path in our younger years. Again, when we are stressed, we do not behave as we usually do. Honestly, how many people have stolen something from a store before? For many, the theft was because there was a stressful event making us believe we needed the item. This is a mild example of criminal behaviors as a coping technique. Some of us have been so stressed, robbed people at gunpoint, sold illegal drugs, committed a hate crime, bribed, or blackmailed someone, kidnapped someone, raped someone, and even murdered someone. These crimes are not committed just because someone is stressed; however, some people reacted to the stressful event and found criminal behavior the most viable solution.

The temporary relief from criminal behaviors is exceptionally brief, similar to violent behaviors. Once the act is completed, the stress of being caught sinks in pretty quickly. Using criminal behaviors as a coping skill, we have just replaced one stressful event with another. This is obviously a self-destructive way of managing stress. Like violent behaviors, criminal behaviors lead to jail/prison time, loneliness, and even death.

> *"Crime does not pay, only you pay for your crimes committed."*

~Ashoka

17. GIVING UP

We hate to admit this, but we live in a society of people giving up easily. We have microwave expectations for crock pot goals and dreams. When things do not happen fast enough or exactly how we want it, we give up. Many people believe that giving up is an excellent coping skill. If the event is causing too much stress, let it go, and the stress goes away. Now, sometimes, we must weigh the pros and cons of an event is worth the stress; however, just giving up because we did not get our way is not coping. Admittedly, giving up can give a more prolonged feeling of relief than most destructive coping skills, but whatever we would have gained if we had not given up could have provided a lifetime of comfort. As mentioned earlier, we were not promised a simple life with no obstacles. Much of the time, we must experience some pain to gain something in return. The journey makes everything seem so worthy, and we feel triumphant.

Giving up is not only a destructive coping skill, but it can become a dangerous habit. If, whenever things get too tough, we give up, then we will accomplish nothing. Talk about stress, not being able to accomplish anything in life. Many agree that nothing is worse than regret. If we spend our lives running from the hard stuff and just giving up, we will have nothing to show but regret. Regret is a stressful event that does not always go away.

> *"Do not fear failure but rather,
> fear not trying."*
>
> ~Roy T. Bennett

18. VIRTUAL ESCAPE

The actual world is harsh. It comes with thousands of stressful events. Feeling the need to escape is perfectly normal. We all need to escape now and then. In the 21st century, we have more avenues to escape than I can list. However, if we spend more hours escaping than living in the actual world, we are in trouble. One of the most common escapes today is virtual technology. We do not have to be in person to socialize, shop, play games, have meetings, party, and even have affairs. All we have to do is pull out our smartphones/tablets or sit in front of our PC/Mac, and we have joined a whole alternative world. Let us assume when all this virtual fun was created, we believed it we would use it in moderation. In moderation, these things are useful for temporarily escaping the stresses of reality. Unfortunately, we are not doing these things in moderation; it has become our reality and sadly our lives.

Virtual escapes take us away from the things that truly matter, our family, friends, work, goals, and dreams. We were all put on this earth for a purpose; we cannot fulfill that purpose locked away in a virtual world. Extended virtual escapes lead to broken families, destroyed friendships, lost jobs, and forgotten goals and dreams. Remember, the actual world gives all the pleasures and joy that the virtual world offers, but we have to take the hardships and stress with it. Take your virtual escapes (except for affairs) and have fun, but set boundaries to limit your time there. The longer you are there, we miss you out here.

"OFFLINE is peace of mind."

~Wild Woman Sisterhood

19. SELF-HARM/SELF-INJURY

Self-harm is drastically growing in popularity as a coping skill. Make no mistake; self-harm is a destructive coping skill. Self-harm is hurting oneself on purpose in attempts to regulate emotions during a stressful event. Usually, self-harm is not a suicide attempt but a dangerous way of trying to control emotional pain. Self-harm includes:

- Cutting
- Burning
- Scratching
- Carving into the skin
- Punching or hitting oneself
- Pulling out hair
- Piercing the skin unprofessionally
- Picking at wounds

Self-harm seems like it provides relief, but it just switches the stressful event from emotional pain to physical pain. Many of us would agree, that at times, physical pain is more tolerable than emotional pain. We all want to avoid or get through emotional pain as much as possible. Unfortunately, some of us will attempt to avoid it at all costs, hence the need to harm oneself physically. Like criminal behaviors, we trade one stressful event for another stressful event, the physical pain and fear of someone finding out.

    Self-harm leads to worsened depression, anxiety, and other mental disorders. This can cause infections in the body. Also, self-harm can cause unintentional suicide. There have been several cases where self-injury leads to bleeding out, or an infection that spread to vital organs, loss of consciousness, and finally death. A significant factor in self-harm as a coping skill is it often cannot be stopped cold turkey. An individual feels they need to self-harm to survive. We must replace the self-harm coping skills with a different and constructive coping skill that offers a similar relief. This can take time to determine, so in the meantime, the self-harm continues. We must remember that those who commit self-harm are trying to cope and survive; we need to offer support, understanding, and options.

> *"Behind every scar there is an untold story..."*
>
> ~Syed Nasir Khalid

20. SUICIDE

Suicide is one of the top ten leading causes of death in the United States; unfortunately, it is also a global problem we need to fight. Suicide is a finite coping skill, which means there is no coming back or a chance to have a change of mind. When we consider suicide as an option to cope with stress, we feel we have exhausted all other options and possibilities. When feeling suicidal, it co-exists with depression, anxiety, and other mental disorders, so not seeing other options can feel like being in a deep black hole all alone with no way out. It is usually not realized that a mental disorder makes it seem like there are no other options. When a suicidal individual confides in someone else, they learn other possibilities they could not see. Now, whether they will try these new options is another issue. So, the inability to find other solutions to stressful events makes suicide a viable coping skill.

Many consider suicide the most selfish act a person can make. Taking one's own life leaves loved ones alone and confused, and many things left unfinished. This takes away the opportunity to try any other coping skills. Suicide takes life and destroys lives. We should not consider suicide a coping skill, but it is for many people. We must speak up if we consider suicide and watch for the signs of others considering suicide. The possibilities, options, and solutions to stressful events are limitless; some of us need a little extra help to see it.

> *"When people kill themselves,*
> *they think they're ending the pain,*
> *but all they're doing is passing it on*
> *to those they leave behind."*

~ Jeannette Walls

CONSTRUCTIVE COPING SKILLS

21. POSITIVE ATTITUDE

We have heard it a thousand times, the importance of our attitude. We may tire of hearing it, but it is true. Our attitude influences our behavior. Think of a time when the atmosphere at the dinner table was uncomfortable; now remember what everyone's attitude was at the dinner table? Did the attitudes influence everyone's behavior, which made the atmosphere uncomfortable? We will go with YES! If our attitude influences our behavior, then a positive attitude will influence our behavior to be positive. This is a coping skill that will offer lasting relief.

When we experience a stressful event, our attitude usually becomes negative and pessimistic. So, it is not surprising that our behavior and our environment become negative as well. The stressful event is already causing havoc in our life; we need some happiness ASAP! In most situations, the only thing you can control is yourself. As hard as it may be, it is up to you to control your attitude and make it positive, even in the darkest moments.

The question continually burning in our brain is, "How do we have a positive attitude in stressful times?" The answer is simple, but not always simple to do. Here is the answer... BRING POSITIVITY INTO OUR LIVES. We do this by reaching out to the positive people in our life, positive input data in our minds daily (daily affirmation books), showing kindness to other so we get it in return, focus on the good things happening (no matter how small), practice positive self-talk, treat ourselves, and smile. This is a concise list, but doing things that make us feel good about ourselves gives us a positive attitude. This is a proactive coping technique, which means we must put forth an effort for it to work. Our attitude is positive, so we can do this.

> *"Attitude is a little thing that makes a big difference."*
>
> ~Winston Churchill

22. RELAXATION

Stress is the opposite of relaxation. When stressed, our muscles tense up, breathing becomes rapid, our heart rate increases, our stomach hurts, we get a headache, and so much more. We are many things in that moment, but relaxed is not one of them. When relaxed, our muscles are loose, breathing is slow and steady, our heart rate decreases, digestion improves, aches and pains subside and so much more. When relaxed, it is easier to think, decide, get things done, eat healthy, and take good care of ourselves. Relaxation is the key to staying healthy during stressful events.

This can be very difficult to manipulate our body to relax during a stressful event. Involuntary responses cause our body to react as discussed earlier.

So, we must do voluntary actions to make our body relax while being stressed. First, we need to stop and recognize that our body is not in a relaxed state but is responding to the stress. So, we have to stop and do an internal and mental check in with ourselves. Then we introduce external variables to our body to manipulate it to relax.

- Deep breathing exercises to slow down breathing
- Stretching, yoga, or warm bath to loosen the muscles
- Meditation to control racing or negative thoughts
- Listening to music to distract from all the chaos
- Journaling to get all the negativity on the inside to the outside

And more…

Relaxation is a proactive coping technique in which we have to put in some effort. Luckily, things that help us relax are things we enjoy, so we are further likely to do them. If we are relaxed, we can handle a stressful event in our path.

> *"Sometimes the most productive thing you can do is relax."*
>
> ~ Mark Black

23. EXERCISE

For some of us, the longest four-letter word is EXERCISE. Let us be realistic, who has the time, energy, and discipline to exercise regularly? Surely not a person dealing with a stressful event. Here is the deal, exercise relieves stress. This is a proven fact. Exercise releases endorphins, which are feel-good neurotransmitters in the brain. Therefore, if we want to reduce our stress and survive the stressful event, we have to make time, find the energy, and get disciplined to exercise. We find the time to get ice cream, see a movie with buttery popcorn, and lay in bed a couple of extra hours on the weekend. If we can do all that, then we can exercise.

Exercise is any physical activity that is repetitive and provides conditioning to the body for fitness. When we think of exercise, we think of running miles, lifting weights for hours, and taking part in workout classes. Physical activity could be dancing around the room, cleaning the house, playing outside with family, walking around the neighborhood, taking the steps at work, and a million other active things. Getting our body moving will release the endorphins and warm up the body to help it relax. Creating an exercise routine will help reduce stress and allow us to handle future stress.

> *"When it comes to health and well-being, regular exercise is about as close to a magic potion as you can get."*
>
> ~ Thích Nhất Hạnh

24. EAT HEALTHY

We are what we eat. What does that really mean? This means the energy in our food becomes our energy. The nutrients in our food become the nutrients fueling our body. The fiber in our food allows us to feel full or still hungry. Whatever the food has to offer, that is all we are going to get. We all love a delicious candy bar, especially when stressed; however, a candy bar has very little energy, so we only get a temporary energy boost, and then we crash. In contrast, an apple is full of slow-release energy, which can last us most of the day. When stressed, our body and mind will go into survival mode. Which means we need all the external help we can get to calm our internal self.

Eating healthy does not mean we can only eat rice cakes, leafy vegetables, and fruit. Most foods can be healthy and offer energy, nutrients, and fiber if eaten in moderation. We do not have to give up red meat to be healthy, but we need to limit the amount of red meat we eat. We need to provide our body what it needs to handle all the stress that it endures. To eat healthier, we can review the nutritional facts, look at serving size, calories, saturated fat, sodium, fiber, and sugar. If the serving size is small, but these other numbers are high, this is not the healthiest option. We can also look at the list of ingredients, the fewer the ingredients, the better.

We are all different sizes, shapes, metabolism levels and activity levels, so research the number of calories or sodium works best for you. We are not meant to live to eat, but eat to live. Let us give our body what it requires to live.

> *"You can't always control what goes on outside, but you can always control what goes on inside."*

~Wayne Dwyer

25. TIME MANAGEMENT

Did you know it stresses us the most when we feel like we are running out of time? Most of the time, when we are running out of time, it is our fault. Time is a very limited resource, but we need it to function in our daily lives. In our lives today, we have a slew of deadlines, scheduled appointments, to-dos on our TO-DOs list, and trying to fit in other people's schedules. We are running around like chickens with our heads cut off, and then we have the audacity to wonder why we are so stressed. Sometimes stress comes at our own hand and really could be avoided. Time management is a proactive coping skill that requires making an effort to plan ahead. This reduce the chances of having a stressful event.

As mentioned above, time is a limited resource, so we need to be better at manipulating our time to our benefit.

- Use a planner or To-Do-List to track all that needs to be done. Do not abandon tasks but be realistic in setting the schedule.
- Set time limits for each task and once the time is up, move on. Otherwise, the entire day could be thrown off schedule.

☐ Use other resources, even other people. Delegate tasks to other people when at home, work, or even grocery shopping.

☐ Prioritize, put the biggest and most important tasks early in the day, and then work your way down to the smallest and easiest tasks.

☐ Audit our time to make sure we are doing what truly needs to be done and eliminating unnecessary things.

Be sure to include rest, fun, and relaxing time in our schedules to ensure we are doing self-care. There are a million things we can do to improve our time management. We need to find what works best for our lifestyle and incorporate it. Stress can disappear when we feel organized, on-time, and in control.

> *"Either you run the day OR the day runs you."*
>
> ~Jim Rohn

26. HOBBIES

When we are stressed, our brain stops functioning properly, and we forget that there is such a thing called... FUN. Just because we are in a stressful event does not mean life stops, and it dooms us to an eternity of misery. Hobbies are the activities we do at leisure for pleasure. There is no better time for pleasure than when we are struggling with stress. A hobby is great for keeping ourselves busy and distracted positively. Many times, focusing on the stressful event makes things worse, so a temporarily pleasurable distraction can be very beneficial.

People have said hobbies are a waste of time. However, we waste time on things that bring absolutely no benefits to our lives every day, such as complaining, gossiping, and procrastinating. Hobbies get us out and active, teach us a new skill, and increases our confidence. To find the best hobby, we need to look at our interests, passions, and dreams. There are several hobbies and activities that will give us what we are searching for; it takes time and initiative to find it. The only requirement is that the chosen hobby is fun.

"A hobby a day keeps the doldrums away."

~Phyllis McGinley

27. REST

Stress takes a toll on the human body. As the stressful event continues, we fight to keep doing everything we can to resolve it or resist it. This takes an even more significant toll on the body. Sometimes, the best defense to a stressful event is to rest or sleep to allow the body to recover and recuperate to continue the fight another day. Many of us worry that if we take the time to rest, the stress will take over, and we will lose. One of life's greatest lessons is learning when not to fight. This can be a hard concept to understand, especially since we are hard-wired to always fight for what we want. This is little known that we can still be in the fight while not putting up a fight. So, let us stop, lay down, sleep, or just rest.

As we have already discussed, a distraction from stress can be very beneficial. Sleep is a great distraction. Now it can be challenging to get the body to relax enough to rest in the course of a stressful event. Try some calming remedies, such as drinking tea, essential oils, taking a hot bath or shower, listen to soothing music, meditate, or anything that helps to relax. Allowing the mind and the body to take a break gives the opportunity to enable other variables to affect the stressful event. As we all know, sometimes stressful events can be resolved on their own.

> *"Almost everything will work again if you unplug it for a few minutes... Including You."*

~Anne Lamott

28. SOCIAL SUPPORT

Humans are not meant to be alone. This is the reason Eve was created for Adam. When we were born, the doctor place on our mother's chest as soon as possible for that human connection. Sometimes we are stressed because we are trying to master this journey alone. This is another example of a stressful event of our own making. Whenever we are struggling or experiencing problems, we should ask for help. We do not want to be a burden on others. Yet, when the people we care about are in trouble, we can quickly jump to their aid. This is so hypocritical and unfair to those who love and care about us.

When we are struggling or having problems, we must allow our loved ones to step in and give us support. Most stressors are too big to fight alone. Loved ones can provide us with suggestions, help us complete tasks, be a sounding board, and be a shoulder to lean on when needed.

Many of us have been brainwashed into believing that asking for help is a sign of weakness. This is a myth; it takes great courage and strength to admit when something is too much and request support. We cannot allow our pride to cause us more stress than we are already struggling with. Call your family, text a friend, email a coworker, tap a stranger on the shoulder, then ask for help. Believe it or not, many of our loved ones are just waiting for the opportunity to be our support. We do not have to struggle in silence; speak up. Humanity, we are not meant to journey through life alone.

"When 'I' is replaced by 'We';
even 'Illness becomes 'Wellness'."

~Author Unknown

29. JOURNALING/VLOGGING

Journaling is as old as time, but vlogging is new and prime. Both are therapeutic techniques that serve the same purpose. They allow us to get all the negativity, racing thoughts, confusion, pessimistic self-talk from inside our heads to the outside world. Journaling/Vlogging is a form of solitary therapy, which means the therapist is the paper or video. The goal is to process our thoughts and emotions tangibly to go back and review it later or metaphorically throw it away.

Many of us struggle with the concept of writing/taping our innermost thoughts and emotions. There is the fear that someone else will discover them. Someone could discover many things about us if they want, but these coping skills give us an outlet when our social support is not available. In a perfect world, we could reach out to our loved ones or therapist anytime for help, but that is not our reality. Occasionally we are stressed, and the only person we have is ourselves. This is the time to take out that notebook or recorder and release all the turmoil on the inside. This does not have to be pretty or even make sense, its purpose is to act as a release. Sharing these with others or reviewing them immediately is a personal choice. Let us allow the journal/vlog to be our social support in those times of need.

> *"Journaling: Paying attention to the inside for the purpose of Living Well from the inside out."*

~ Lee W.

30. ART CREATIVITY

It is widely believed that art and creativity can foster mental well-being and healing. Art has been used to treat stress by either reviewing others' work or creating one's own work. This helps us cope with stress, increase our self-esteem, and explore our thoughts and emotions. Art and creativity are not about being gifted in art, but taking the time to find beauty and joy in things. Our daily bustle makes it difficult to stop and smell the roses or enjoy the moment. Studies have shown that stress and anxiety can stem from us focusing too much on the future. Art and creativity are techniques used to keep us focused on the present. Art and creativity are quiet, calming, meditative, and soothes symptoms of stress.

Try several mediums of art, such as crayons, paper, paint, collage, clay, and other art supplies to try art and creativity. Experimenting with several mediums to determine which we connect with and enjoy the most. We can color a picture, draw our own image, sculpt something, create jewelry, decorate something we own, make a collage, or analyze and admire unfamiliar works from other artists. Whatever we choose, we want to spark some emotion or thought about the experience. Hopefully, it will be something we want to repeat. Focusing on the present is challenging, but art and creativity provide an anchor to keep us in the moment.

> *"Art is not always about pretty things. It's about who we are, what happened to us, and how our lives are affected."*
>
> ~Elizabeth Brown

31. MUSIC & DANCE

Music and dance focus on body movement and physical healing. This is a therapeutic interaction between music and the body. Studies have shown that music can be so relaxing it can lessen the feeling of pain and distress. Dance provides an outlet for expressing pain and distress through movement and the use of the space in the area. The combination of the two provides the brain's stimulation from music and stimulation of the body from dance. This becomes a multi-sensory coping skill involving the auditory, tactile, and visual senses. Music allows us to experience our range of emotions, which is very cathartic to feel emotional connections, process how to overcome challenges, and get through stressful emotions. Dance allows us to express what we gained from music in our own unique way. Dance gives us our individuality of expression and releases feel-good hormones like dopamine and endorphins.

To receive the benefits of music, we have to find the songs that influence our lives. We want songs that stimulate our body, feelings, emotions, questions, and thoughts. An eclectic approach to music is the most therapeutic. Listen to different genres, artists, and albums until we create a unique therapeutic playlist.

Then we dance to the music, developing and creating body movements to express what we are experiencing and feeling. An additional step to these coping skills is to record our performance and relive it again later. Music and dance are about staying present and feeling the moment. Go create a musical experience!

> *"Dancing and music can cure things medication never will."*
>
> ~William Blanco May

32. GARDENING

Gardening is not for all of us, but it can be so tranquil and rewarding. If we look at it from an evolutionary perspective, our ancestors spent most of the day planting and growing and relaxing their minds and spirits. Becoming one with the earth has been said to be very peaceful. Gardening can be indoors with potted plants or outdoors with new seeds or established plants. Both options offer the therapeutic activity of sustaining something that can be enjoyed for extended periods. Gardening works because it allows us to take the negative energy from being stressed and convert into positive energy that builds something beautiful.

For those who do not have a green thumb, we can still enjoy the benefits of gardening by keeping self-sustaining plants around the home for us to see and be around. Otherwise, let us roll up our sleeves, get our hand dirty, and plant those seeds to watch the fruit of our labor blossom into a land of beauty. Remember, the mere presence of plants naturally soothes us and reduces our stress. Whether we buy some seeds or a plant, let us interact with the plants in our lives to help us cope with our next stressful event.

> *"We might think we are nurturing our garden, but of course it's our garden that is really nurturing us."*
>
> ~Jenny Uglow

33. NATURE

Camping, hiking, fishing, and bird watching are all things we do in nature for enjoyment. Spending time in nature is also a coping skill to deal with stress. The environment plays a significant role in our mental well-being. What we hear, see, and feel can change our mood and how our endocrine and nervous system function. The comfort we get from a natural breeze, the vitamin D we get from the blazing sun, and the fresh aroma we get from breathing fresh air; reduces our fear, anger, and stress. Mother nature is a holistic remedy to stress and anxiety.

Coping through nature is easy. All we have to do is step outside of the house or office. We can eat lunch in the park, take a break at work, sit on a bench outside, do our exercises on a nature trail, sit in our backyard to read, decorate our office with nature paraphernalia, or drive through the country with the windows down. There are so many ways we can incorporate time to commune with nature into our schedule. Let us become one with mother nature and heal our stress holistically, the way it was intended.

> *"At some point in life, the world's beauty becomes enough. You do not need to photograph, paint, or even remember it. It is enough."*
>
> ~Toni Morrison

34. EMOTIONAL SUPPORT ANIMAL

Most people in the world would benefit from an emotional support animal's (ESA) constant companionship, especially when stressed. An ESA is an animal companion that helps ease at least one aspect of a physical or psychiatric disability. An ESA helps us be more social, feel safer, feel comforted, and increase our sense of purpose. They help with loneliness and become an added member of our social support. Research has shown that an ESA can speed up physical and emotional healing. An ESA helps us cope by just being there for us. These animals do not need any special training; their mere presence reduces our stress level. The act of petting an animal has an even greater effect on mental well-being. ESAs are another holistic approach to healing.

ESAs take some responsibility on our part. We must care for another living creature. The act of caring for something is also a therapeutic way of coping. This gives us a sense of purpose and control when we feel we have little purpose or control. An ESA does not have to be registered to qualify as an ESA to you personally, but the ESA must be certified and registered for legal purposes. ESAs can be any animal but are usually one of the following, dog, cat, bird, reptile, rabbit, ferret, hamster, and other furry friends. ESAs can come from breeders, the humane society, friends giving away pets, animal care and control, and pet stores. The most crucial factor about the ESA is that he/she helps us with our struggles and stress. There is nothing quite like a cute furry face to make us smile when the world is on our shoulders.

> *"Sometimes the best medicine is a pet who thinks their love can cure you."*
>
> ~Author Unknown

35. AROMATHERAPY/ESSENTIAL OILS

There is nothing like walking into a room, and the aroma catches our nose, and our body involuntarily relaxes. We suddenly have a gut instinct that everything is going to be all right. Our sense of smell has the strongest relationship with memory. Our sense of smell can trigger memories, feelings, and send a chill through the body. Aromatherapy uses natural plant extracts through holistic healing to promote mental well-being. The natural plant extracts are essential oils. Aromatherapy helps with stress, sleep, relaxation, immune system, weight management, respiratory health, energy and so much more.

Aromatherapy diffuses the oils into the air so that when we smell it, then the extracts from the plant enter our body. These extracts came naturally from plants and were used by our ancestors for healing and well-being. The diffusing of essential oils also makes the room/office smell pleasant for others to enjoy. To diffuse an essential oil, we would have to purchase a diffuser found online or in-stores. We can also wear diffuser jewelry, which is fashionable, portable, and will diffuse the essential oils throughout the day.

Another medium for essential oils to enter the bloodstream is through topical application. The essential oils can be rubbed on the bottom of the feet, which has the most pores and will get it in the bloodstream faster. We can apply it to the wrist, neck, behind the ears, and any part of the body in pain. We can purchase essential oils online, in-stores, and at reputable distributors. This is a coping technique that does the job on its own.

"Aromatherapy conveys the concept of healing with aromatic substances."
~Robert Tisserand

36. BOOKS/MOVIES

It can be so fun to get caught up in someone else's drama for a while. The need to escape our stressors is very typical. Books/Movies invites us to another world to experience things through various characters. These coping skills offer a chance to process different feelings, emotions, and scenarios vicariously through someone else. The storylines reveal different outcomes for various situations that we may have experienced. Books/Movies allow us to focus on the characters' issues and forget our own problems for a while. This is a coping skill most of us do daily and enjoy, so this is a more effortless skill to implement.

Finding a book/movie is like finding music; we should try all the genres and determine what makes the greatest impact. Again, it is best if we are eclectic with the books we read and the movies we watch. A crucial factor for this coping skill is to step out of our comfort zone. To get the full treatment, we have to be willing to try books/movies that we usually never consider or ignore because of fear of what it might trigger. Self-help books, daily devotionals, inspirational podcasts, the bible, and spiritual movies should be in our repertoire of books/movies. Let us sit back, relax, and enjoy the show.

> *"A reader lives a thousand lives before he dies... The man who never reads lives only one."*
>
> ~George R. R. Martin

37. BATH/SHOWER

Calgon, Take Me Away!! We have all had those days where we want to come home and wash away the stressors of the day. Baths/showers help our body to relax. The heat from the water loosens the muscles, aromatherapy from the soap calms the mind, the showerhead's pulse massages the body, and the body washing symbolically washes the day off. Since we bathe regularly, our body can crave a bath/shower in times of distress.

Nighttime baths/showers can be therapeutic. This is not necessarily about getting clean, but releasing the filth from the day. Most of us sleep so much better when we take a bath/shower before bed. A bath/shower makes us feel new. A tip for nighttime bathing is to use Johnson's Bedtime Moisture Wash for babies. The calming and sleep-inducing effects of this wash work on adults as well, with a higher dosage. We should treat our bath/shower like a spa treatment and focus on soothing ourselves.

"When in doubt, take a bath."

~Mae West

38. STRESS TOYS

We are never too old to play with toys. Stress toys we designed for us to release tension and to find focus. Restlessness is a sign of stress. Keeping our hands busy helps us to feel in control. Whenever kids get overly anxious or cannot concentrate, we give them a toy to catch their attention, keep them focused, and keep them occupied. Stress toys work the same for us; when stressed, they take our attention away from the stressor. They keep us focused on what our hand is doing or on what is in front of us. They keep us busy completing the task at hand in the stress's midst. Stress toys improve mental health and treat carpal tunnel syndrome, arthritis, and boost blood circulation.

A stress toy could be anything. Toys and items around the house or something bought from a store. The key measure is that it makes us feel calmer when playing with it in our hands. Stress toys:
- Fidget Spinners
- Silly Putty
- Play Foam
- Squishy Balls
- Magnetic Balls
- DIY Toys

All these toys have in common are that they all force the hand to stay in motion, which is resistant to restlessness. Idle hands are the devil's playground.

> *"So, you mean to tell me a stress ball isn't for throwing at people who stress you out?"*
>
> ~Minions

39. LAUGH

Some say laughter is the best medicine. Gladly, this is true because we do not need a prescription to laugh. When we laugh, it releases endorphins, cortisol levels are reduced and we breathe in oxygen-rich air, our lungs, muscles, and heart are stimulated. Laughter can even add years to our life. No wonder laughter reduces stress. Laughter is involuntary when we have been amused by something. Fake laughing as a voluntary response still has a positive effect on us. Sometimes we have to fake it till we make it.

When stressed, sometimes it hurts too much to laugh. We feel a hundred miles from happiness, and fake laughter seems impossible. When we are in so much pain that we cannot laugh voluntarily; we must introduce an external variable that will trigger involuntary laughter. Since we are all different, our sense of humor is different, so we have to find things amusing to us.

We can do a few things, watch a Stand-Up comedian, watch a comedy movie, listen to funny jokes, reminisce on funny memories, play with kids or pets, and be silly with ourselves. Once the laughter starts, it is difficult to contain. Laughter is one of the most therapeutic coping skills. The effects can be temporary or lasting, but either way, it can be practiced a million times over again.

> *"I have seen what a laugh can do. It can transform almost unbearable into something bearable, even hopeful."*
>
> ~Bob Hope

40. SMILE & BREATHE

Stress can take us out of our zone and cause us to do something we usually would not do. In these situations, we first need to stop, smile, and then breathe. When we smile, our brain releases feel-good neurotransmitters like dopamine, serotonin, endorphins and neuropeptides to fight the stress. Once we have found a spark of joy, we have to breathe to trigger our logical thinking. Smiling and breathing can take control of our body and force it into a different direction. An initial stress reaction can be to do impulsive behaviors. A simple smile and breathing exercise can stop all impulsivity in its tracks.

This coping skill can initially be difficult because we do not recognize that we are not smiling when we are stressed. Hence the first step in this three-step process is to stop. We must take the time to realize what our body is doing, specifically our face. Once we have mastered this skill of fixing our face to a smile, we must remember to breathe.

How many times have been so stressed or angered and realized we have stopped breathing? We did not stop breathing to cause ourselves to pass out, but we stopped breathing calm and stable breaths. We either breathe too fast, almost hyperventilating, or we breathe too deep and slow. To control breathing, we need to find a consistent beat to follow. We can use the second's hands on a clock, the rhythm of counting to ten, or the beat of tapping our foot. Once we have mastered controlling our breathing, we can handle any stressful event in our path.

> *"Life is like a mirror. Smile at it and it smiles back at you."*
>
> ~Peace Pilgrim

41. REFRAMED THINKING

Many times, we allow things to become stressors because of our perspective of the situation. It is genuinely beneficial when we can see things from more than one lens. Even the most optimistic person could benefit from reframing their thoughts to see another viewpoint. Our perspectives are shaped by our values, life experiences, assumptions, the current state of mind, and several other variables. This means that any situation can be viewed as a crisis about to erupt. Reframing our thinking involves taking the stressor or stressful event and analyzing it within its actual context.

This is another coping skill that can be tricky and will take time to master. However, once we have this skill, it will change every aspect of our lives. Scenario: The boss asks us to do a task outside our job description. She is not offering any incentives and has only given us 48 hours to complete it.

42. INITIAL PERSPECTIVE

The boss does not appreciate all that we already do and is steadily adding more work. She does not give us the time she gives the other team members. The least she could do is give something for this extra work. Feeling so stressed and feel we should not have to do this.

43. ALTERNATE PERSPECTIVE

The boss knows she cannot rely on anyone else on the team to get this done. I must let her know some other tasks will be done a little later because of this new project. Wow, these new skills from doing this project will look great on the resume.

The same situation from two different viewpoints. One became a stressful event, and the other became an opportunity for advancement. Again, this skill takes time to learn and master. The first step is to ask other people we trust their perspective on the situation. Then we take the time to reframe our thinking based on the feedback we receive. This coping skill takes a massive amount of effort in the short-term, but the long-term outcomes are priceless.

"If you don't like something change it; If you can't change it, change the way you think about it."

~Mary Engelbreit

44. FIND RESOLUTION

Everyone hates it when someone falls apart and plays the victim. Admittedly, we all have done it from time to time. We find ourselves in a stressful event, and we cry and whine about how unfair life can be. Life is not fair; we should have learned this lesson at a very young age. The problem is that we see the stressful event as overpowering us and taking control of everything. We become a victim to circumstance. In reality, we need to get off the floor and figure out the solution to the problems. We need to take our control back and determine what our outcome will be. No one has to be a victim of any circumstance. Take control over our lives and our destiny by making good choices. The solution to all stressors and stressful events is out there; we have to find it.

Finding a solution can be more challenging than it seems. The trick to this coping skill is that we have to put on our thinking cap in the storm's midst. We all know we would like to sleep in the storm's midst, but we must work. The simplest way to start this process is to brainstorm. List out all the potential solutions, no matter how silly or impossible it may seem. We can also brainstorm the pros and cons of the stressful event which could help us reframe our thinking. Get as many options and as much information down on paper as we can. Then we eliminate fluff and focus on the genuine possibilities. There will be at least one possibility that will either resolve the situation or reduce the situation's impact. We must do the work.

"If the challenge exists, so must the solution."

~Rona Mlnarik

45. BE GRATEFUL

Stress Sucks! We all hate everything about it, and none of us wants to experience it. However, things could always be worse. One of the most looked over coping skill is to be grateful. We can always find someone that worse off than we are. When we acknowledge all that we have and accomplished, the stress does not seem like a heavy burden. We need to remember, if we never have bad things happen, then we cannot fully appreciate the good things.

Gratefulness should be ingrained in who we are. We should appreciate all the kindness, benefits, and even the obstacles in our lives. These are the things that make us who we are. Truth be told, being grateful does not come easy for many of us. There are many ways we can practice being grateful:

- Remember the bad things and all we have overcome
- Keep a journal of our grace, gifts, benefits, and good things
- Say prayers of gratitude

- Create visual reminders of what to be grateful for
- Give back to others or pay it forward

And much more

Being grateful is just the tip of the iceberg. Behaving gratefully will significantly reduce the impact of any stressor that crosses our path.

> *"The more you are grateful for what you have. The more you will have to be grateful for."*
>
> ~Zig Ziglar

46. PRAYER/MEDITATION

Prayer changes things. Some things we cannot control, and we need supernatural help. Prayer is a one-on-one conversation between us and our higher power. Prayer is being thankful for all that has been giving and asking for help with our daily struggles. Regardless if we are religious, faith-based, or spiritual, whatever we believe in is always with us. As mentioned before, we were never meant to take this journey of life alone. The higher power we believe in is always by our side. Prayer brings us out of the flesh's restraints and confinement and allows us to enter the supernatural for guidance and support. Prayer is the only coping skill that never fails.

Religion has made prayer seem like a complex and complicated event. It is actually very simple. Like we speak to each other, we can go to our higher power and have a conversation. Once we give our stressors to our higher power, we have to let it go. It no longer belongs to us, and in time we will see it disappear. Our higher power created each of us with a purpose and wants to hear from us no matter what. The goal is for this to be comfortable to practice and becomes a part of our daily lives. We know what prayer can do, so let us do it.

Meditation has been used in many cultures and is well known to have psychological benefits. The simple act of slowing down, focusing on your breathing, and clearing your mind can help reduce stress.

> *"Prayers don't have to be long and eloquent. They need only come from a sincere and humble heart."*
>
> ~Author Unknown

47. SEEK PROFESSIONAL HELP

When we continuously feel stressed and overwhelmed, even after utilizing multiple other coping skills, this could be a sign of a more deeply rooted issue. In this situation, it is highly recommended we seek professional help from a Mental Health Professional (MHP). Receiving support from an MHP is normal and quite healthy. There are many stigmas around mental health services. Speaking with a counselor about a stressful event is the same as talking to a friend, except this friend is not biased, cannot tell anyone your secrets, and can offer guidance that has been proven to help. Working with a psychiatrist for medication is the same as working with your primary care physician for medication. Everyone should try counseling at least once. We never know what we might learn about ourselves.

Many of us have considered trying mental health services, but we have no idea how to get started. Most MHPs accept insurance, so we can always contact our insurance provider for a list of covered MHPs in the area. We can also find MHPs online from websites they subscribe to advertise their services, such as Psychology Today, Good Therapy and many others. Telehealth has become a big industry in the field of mental health services. We can do counseling via live chat, telephone, or video from the comforts of home. Many companies are offering these services, such as BetterHelp Inc, TalkSpace and many others. There are so many options for mental health services; we cannot let our fears or concerns stand in the way. Let us begin our journey to better emotional and mental health.

> *"Counseling has to do with intuition, with work on oneself, with the quietness of one's mind, and the openness of one's heart."*
>
> ~Ram Dass

48. KIDS & STRESS

In the 21st Century, kids are dealing with more and more adult problems and responsibilities. It is hard just to be a kid these days. Family struggles are being put on their shoulders. Cartoons are even dealing with adult issues. These changes mean that kids are struggling and feeling just as stressed as adults. Some adults cannot fathom what a kid would be stressed over. However, we cannot dismiss this growing pandemic. Kids are exhibiting all the signs of stress and anxiety at younger and younger ages. We must address these issues head-on. We need to show our kids they are not alone. Teach them that stress is an ordinary part of life and to use constructive coping skills to handle the pressure. Stress can quickly overtake kids. Remember, we learn coping skills, and we want our kids to learn and practice the very best.

"Your kid's not a bad kid, they're responding to something, and we have to figure out what."

~Jess Sherman

49. FAMILY TIME

Our kids will never tell us this, but on some level, they enjoy family time. As they get older, they resist it, but we cannot quit. Family time creates the bonds and connections of love and friendship amongst family members. This quality time with family is a coping skill in itself. We give our kids a time where nothing from the outside world can get to them, even if it is only temporary. We provide a venue where our kids feel comfortable enough to open up about some of their struggles and stressors. Family time provides security, family values, improves confidence, and much more. Spend this time having fun with games, movies, karaoke, jokes, food, and anything that brings joy. We only have 18 years of mandatory family time, and that time goes by fast. Let us make sure our kids know they are part of a loving family unit and be a family unit they can be proud to be a member.

> *"Family Time is sacred time and should be protected and respected."*
>
> ~Boyd K. Packer

50. FAMILY PHOTOS

Going down memory lane and looking at photos can be very sentimental. When our kids are stressed, they need a little of our sentiment. Family photos can boost our kid's self-esteem. They show who came before us and provides a special connection. Kids like to feel connected and grounded, especially when they think their life is in chaos. Being connected to your own story has a powerful impact. Seeing photos of ancestors, family, and themselves from past to present offers a glimpse into how their world and how they were shaped. Connecting with family photos may seem like a minute coping skill, but it makes an enormous impact on our lives and our children's lives.

"The best thing about a picture is that it never changes, even when the people in it do."

~Andy Warhol

51. PEP TALKS

We have to talk to our kids. If we do not talk to them, who will? All the wrong people will happily tell our kids everything wrong. We must be a sounding board for our kids. There should be times when our kids can talk to us and confide in us about what is happening in their life without consequence. Kids are out here struggling and fighting adult battles alone because it scares them to be honest with us. There is a time and place when our kids should have a healthy fear and respect toward us, and there is a moment and place they should feel safe to come to us with anything. We tell our kids to come to us when they are in trouble, but then we punish them for it. Pep talks are another we can teach our kids how to cope with stress. We listen to what they are going through and then provide them with support and options for dealing with it. Let us be the voice of reason in our kid's head.

"Children will listen to you after they feel listened to."

~Jane Nelson

52. EXTENDED FAMILY & FRIENDS

Let us be realistic; no matter how much we talk to our kids, there are some things they will not tell us. This is the reason it is essential to provide our kids with strong social support. There must be other people that we trust that our kids can trust. Kids need to know their extended family to ensure that they see the village members there to support and protect them. Kids need to have their own friends, but we need to know these friends and their families. Social support is as crucial for our kids as for us, if not more. The feeling of being surrounded by love can make a stressful event feel like a blip on the radar. Love is the most powerful tool we can give our kids in their time of need, but not just our love, everyone's love. We not only need to see the village, but the village must be active in our kid's life.

50 Things to Know

*"Family like branches on a tree,
we all grow in different directions,
yet our roots remain as one."*

~Author Unknown

OTHER HELPFUL RESOURCES

HelpLine: https://helplinedelmor.org/24-hour-crisis-hotline/

National Alliance on Mental Health:
https://www.nami.org/help

Office On Women's Health:
https://www.womenshealth.gov/mental-health/get-help-now

Teen Health & Wellness:
https://teenhealthandwellness.com/static/hotlines

READ OTHER 50 THINGS TO KNOW BOOKS

50 Things to Know to Get Things Done Fast: Easy Tips for Success

50 Things to Know About Going Green: Simple Changes to Start Today

50 Things to Know to Live a Happy Life Series

50 Things to Know to Organize Your Life: A Quick Start Guide to Declutter, Organize, and Live Simply

50 Things to Know About Being a Minimalist: Downsize, Organize, and Live Your Life

50 Things to Know About Speed Cleaning: How to Tidy Your Home in Minutes

50 Things to Know About Choosing the Right Path in Life

50 Things to Know to Get Rid of Clutter in Your Life: Evaluate, Purge, and Enjoy Living

50 Things to Know About Journal Writing: Exploring Your Innermost Thoughts & Feelings

50 Things to Know

Stay up to date with new releases on Amazon:

https://amzn.to/2VPNGr7

50 Things to Know

Please leave your honest review of this book on Amazon and Goodreads. We appreciate your positive and constructive feedback. Thank you.

www.ingramcontent.com/pod-product-compliance
Lightning Source LLC
Chambersburg PA
CBHW070436220526
45466CB00004B/1695